.CLASSICS.
Illustrated®

Homer
THE ILIAD

essay by
Maurice A. Randall
Roxbury Latin School

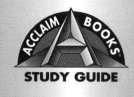

The Iliad
Originally published as Classics Illustrated no. 77

Art by Alex Blum
Cover by Enrique Alcatena

For Classics Illustrated Study Guides
computer recoloring by Twilight Graphics
editor: Madeleine Robins
assistant editor: Valerie D'Orazio
design: Joseph Caponsacco

Dale-Chall R.L.: 9.45

ISBN 1-57848-052-X

Acclaim Books, New York, NY
Printed in the United States

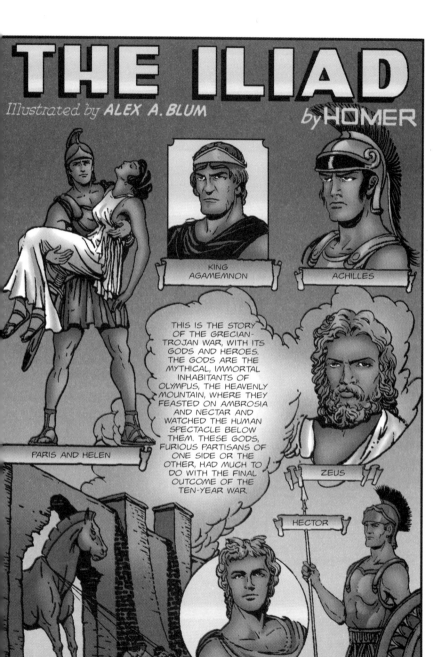

THE ILIAD

Illustrated by **ALEX A. BLUM**

by **HOMER**

KING AGAMEMNON

ACHILLES

PARIS AND HELEN

THIS IS THE STORY OF THE GRECIAN-TROJAN WAR, WITH ITS GODS AND HEROES. THE GODS ARE THE MYTHICAL, IMMORTAL INHABITANTS OF OLYMPUS, THE HEAVENLY MOUNTAIN, WHERE THEY FEASTED ON AMBROSIA AND NECTAR AND WATCHED THE HUMAN SPECTACLE BELOW THEM. THESE GODS, FURIOUS PARTISANS OF ONE SIDE OR THE OTHER, HAD MUCH TO DO WITH THE FINAL OUTCOME OF THE TEN-YEAR WAR.

ZEUS

HECTOR

APOLLO

TYNDAREUS, KING OF SPARTA, PRESENTED HIS DAUGHTER, HELEN, TO THE PRINCES OF GREECE.

YOU MUST SWEAR THAT YOU WILL BE GOOD FRIENDS WITH THE MAN WHOM MY DAUGHTER SHALL CHOOSE FOR HER HUSBAND.

WE DO

HELEN CHOSE MENELAUS, BROTHER OF AGAMEMNON, WHO WAS CHIEF OF ALL THE KINGS OF GREECE.

AFTER A WHILE, HELEN'S FATHER DIED AND MENELAUS BECAME KING OF SPARTA.

MENELAUS AND HELEN LIVED HAPPILY TOGETHER UNTIL THERE CAME TO SPARTA A YOUNG PRINCE, PARIS BY NAME, WHO WAS THE SON OF PRIAM, KING OF TROY.

CRAZED BY HIS LOVE FOR HER, PARIS STOLE HELEN FROM HER HUSBAND.

MENELAUS' BROTHER, AGAMEMNON, CALLED A MEETING OF ALL GREEK LEADERS . . .

YOU PRINCES OF GREECE MUST KEEP YOUR OATH AND HELP MY BROTHER GET BACK THE FAIR HELEN.

WE'LL KEEP OUR OATH.

THUS BEGAN THE WAR BETWEEN THE GREEKS AND THE TROJANS. FOR NINE YEARS, THE GREEKS BESIEGED TROY, BUT THEY COULD NOT BREAK THROUGH THE CITY WALLS. THEY CAME TO BE IN GREAT WANT OF FOOD AND CLOTHES, SO THEY LEFT PART OF THE ARMY TO WATCH THE CITY, AND WITH THE REST THEY WENT FORTH AND DESPOILED OTHER CITIES. THUS CAME ABOUT THE GREAT QUARREL . . . BETWEEN AGAMEMNON AND ACHILLES.

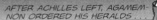

AFTER ACHILLES LEFT, AGAMEMNON ORDERED HIS HERALDS . . .

GO TO THE TENT OF ACHILLES AND FETCH THE GIRL BRISEIS. AND IF HE'LL NOT LET HER GO, SAY I'LL COME WITH OTHERS TO FETCH HER, AND IT'LL BE THE WORSE FOR HIM.

IN GREAT FEAR AND SHAME, THE HERALDS STOOD BEFORE ACHILLES . . .

DRAW NEAR. TIS NO FAULT OF YOURS THAT YOU ARE COME ON SUCH AN ERRAND.

THE HERALDS WILL REMEMBER THIS DAY WHEN AGAMEMNON SHALL NEED MY HELP AND HE SHALL NOT HAVE IT.

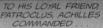

TO HIS LOYAL FRIEND, PATROCLUS, ACHILLES COMMANDED . . .

FETCH BRISEIS FROM HER TENT AND GIVE HER TO THE HERALDS LET THEM BE WITNESSES OF THIS EVIL DEED!

ACHILLES TOLD HIS MOTHER, *THETIS, OF THE PLOT AGAINST HIM . . .

GO TO OLYMPUS . . . TO THE PALACE OF ZEUS** AND ASK HIM TO HELP THE TROJANS SO THAT AGAMEMNON MAY LEARN HOW FOOLISH HE HAS BEEN.

HE'S ATTENDING A TWELVE DAYS' FEAST, BUT I'LL ASK HIM WHEN HE COMES BACK. MEANWHILE, DO YOU SIT STILL AND DO NOT GO FORTH TO BATTLE!

**GOD OF HEAVEN AND EARTH.   *DAUGHTER OF THE SEA.

WHILE ALL THE OTHER GODS SLEPT, ZEUS REMAINED AWAKE THINKING HOW HE MIGHT AID THETIS AND HER SON, ACHILLES.

PERHAPS IF AGAMEMNON THOUGHT HE COULD TAKE THE CITY OF TROY . . . AH, YES, THAT WILL DECEIVE HIM!

THEN ZEUS SUMMONED A DREAM.

GO, DREAM, TO THE TENT OF AGAMEMNON, AND TELL HIM THAT IF HE WILL LEAD HIS ARMY TO BATTLE, HE'LL TAKE THE CITY OF TROY.

THE DREAM TOOK THE FORM OF NESTOR, WHOM AGAMEMNON THOUGHT TO BE THE WISEST OF THE GREEKS, AND STOOD BY THE BEDSIDE OF THE KING AND SAID . . .

WHY DO YOU WASTE YOUR TIME IN SLEEP? ARM THE GREEKS AND LEAD THEM OUT TO BATTLE, FOR YOU'LL TAKE THE CITY OF TROY.

THE KING BELIEVED THAT THIS FALSE DREAM WAS TRUE . . .

WE'RE GOING TO BATTLE AGAINST THE TROJANS. AT LAST, THIS LONG WAR IS GOING TO END.

THE GREEKS AND THE TROJANS MET BEFORE THE WALLS OF THE CITY OF TROY. COUNTLESS WERE THE GREAT AND HEROIC DEEDS DONE THAT DAY. WHILE MANY CHIEFS SHOWED THEMSELVES TO BE BRAVE AND VALIANT MEN, THE MOST SINGULAR AND OUTSTANDING EXPLOITS WERE ACCOMPLISHED BY DIOMED. IN THE MIDST OF THE TERRIFIC ATTACK, AN ARROW HIT HIM IN THE SHOULDER.

AJAX HELD HIS GREAT SHIELD BEFORE HIM, AS IT MIGHT BE A WALL. IT HAD SEVEN FOLDS OF BULL'S HIDE AND ONE FOLD OF BRONZE...

COME NEAR, HECTOR, THAT YOU MAY SEE WHAT MEN WE HAVE AMONG US, WE GREEKS, THOUGH THE GREAT ACHILLES SITS IDLE IN HIS TENT.

DO NOT SPEAK TO M[E] GREAT AJAX, AS TO [A] CHILD. I KNOW ALL TH[E] ARTS OF BATTLE! COME, LET US FIGHT OPENLY, FACE TO FAC[E].

THEN HECTOR THREW HIS SPEAR. THROUGH SIX FOLDS OF BULL-HIDE THE SPEAR PASSED BUT THE SEVENTH STOPPED IT.

AJAX THREW HIS SPEAR. IT PASSED THROUGH HECTOR'S SHIELD AND CAME NEAR KILLING HIM.

THE WARRIORS TOOK FRESH SPEARS AND RAN TOGETHER AS FIERCELY AS LIONS OR WILD BOARS.

THE BATTLE WAS GOING AGAINST HECTOR. A SPEAR POINT HAD GRAZED HIS NECK AND HE BLED. NOW THE WARRIORS TURNED TO SWORDS.

ZEUS TOOK A HAND IN THE STRUGGLE AND ADDRESSED THE GODS AND GODDESSES...

LISTEN AND OBEY! NO ONE OF YOU SHALL HELP EITHER THE GREEKS OR THE TROJANS... AND MARK THIS... IF ANY GOD OR GODDESS DARES TO DO SO, I'LL THROW HIM DOWN INTO THE OUTER DARKNESS!

DOES ANYONE THINK THAT I'M NOT STRONGER THAN ALL OF YOU PUT TOGETHER?

FATHER, WE KNOW RIGHT WELL THAT NONE OF US CAN STAND UP AGAINST YOU. AND YET WE CAN NOT HELP PITYING THE GREEKS, FOR WE FEAR THEY'LL BE ALTOGETHER DESTROYED!

ATHENE WAS HIS DAUGHTER, AND ZEUS LOVED HER BETTER THAN ANY AMONG THE GODS AND GODDESSES, SO HE LISTENED AS SHE SPOKE.

WE'LL NOT HELP THE GREEKS, FOR THIS YOU FORBID. BUT, IF YOU'LL PERMIT, WE'LL GIVE THEM ADVICE.

CONSENTING TO HIS DAUGHTER'S PLAN TO ADVISE THE GREEKS, ZEUS YOKED HIS CHARIOT AND FLEW MIDWAY THROUGH HEAVEN AND EARTH TILL HE CAME TO MT. IDA NEAR TO TROY.

ZEUS SAT DOWN AND WATCHED THE BATTLE. THE TIME HAD COME WHEN HE WOULD KEEP THE PROMISE MADE TO THETIS TO HELP THE TROJANS SO THAT THE GREEKS WOULD FEEL THE ABSENCE OF ACHILLES.

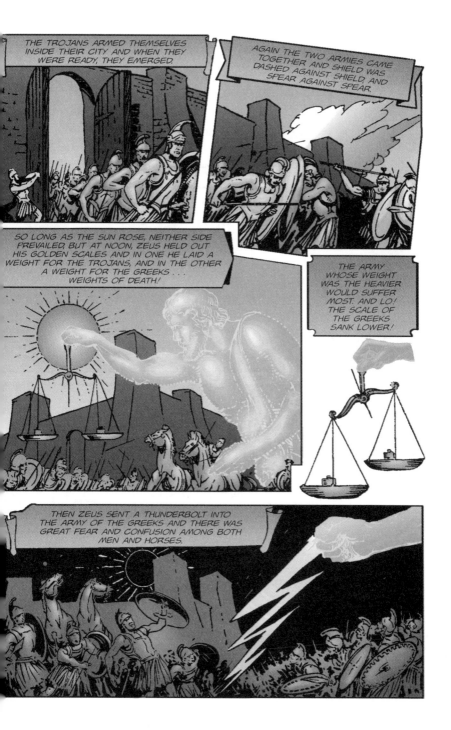

DISPIRITED, THE GREEKS RETREATED TO THE PROTECTION OF THE WALL WHICH THEY HAD BUILT AS A DEFENSE FOR THEIR SHIPS.

KING AGAMEMNON WAS ENCOURAGED BY THE GODDESS HERA TO PERSUADE HIS PEOPLE TO RETURN TO BATTLE.

SHAME ON YOU! WHAT OF YOUR BOASTS THAT ONE OF YOU WOULD BE A MATCH FOR A HUNDRED TROJANS?

IT WAS EASY TO SAY SUCH THINGS WHEN YOU ATE THE FLESH OF BULLOCKS AND DRANK FULL CUPS OF WINE! BUT NOW, A SINGLE TROJAN IS WORTH MORE THAN ALL OF YOU!

WAS THERE EVER A KING WHO HAD SUCH COWARDS FOR HIS PEOPLE?

KING AGAMEMNON'S TALK GAVE THE GREEKS NEW COURAGE AND THEY TURNED AND SET UPON THE TROJANS AGAIN.

THAT NIGHT, HECTOR ADDRESSED THE TROJANS . . .

NIGHT HAS COME AND HINDERED US FROM FINISHING OUR WORK. SOME OF YOU FETCH FUEL THAT WE MAY BURN FIRES AND WATCH THE GREEKS TO SEE WHETHER THEY WILL TRY TO ESCAPE.

TRULY THEY'LL NOT GO IN PEACE. MANY WILL WE KILL. THE REST SHALL CARRY AWAY WOUNDS TO HEAL AT HOME, SO NO MAN MAY COME AGAIN AND TROUBLE THIS CITY OF TROY.

HERALDS SHALL GO TO THE CITY AND PROCLAIM THAT ALL PEOPLE KEEP WATCH, LEST THE ENEMY ENTER THE CITY WHILE WE ARE FIGHTING AT THE SHIPS.

TOMORROW, WE'LL DRIVE THE GREEKS TO THEIR SHIPS . . . AND IF IT MAY BE . . . BURN THESE SHIPS.

A THOUSAND FIRES WERE BURNING, AND BY EACH FIRE SAT FIFTY MEN. AND THE HORSES STOOD BY THE CHARIOTS CHAMPING OATS AND BARLEY. SO THEY ALL WAITED FOR MORNING . . .

THE GREEKS WERE SORELY TROUBLED, BUT NOT ONE WAS MORE SAD THAN KING AGAMEMNON, AS HE SPOKE TO HIS CHIEFS . . .

O, MY FRIENDS, TRULY ZEUS SEEMS TO HATE ME.

ONCE HE PROMISED THAT I SHOULD TAKE THIS CITY OF TROY AND RETURN HOME IN SAFETY. BUT THIS PROMISE HE HAS NOT KEPT!

BEFORE WE PERISH, LET US FLEE TO OUR OWN LAND, FOR TROY WE MAY NOT TAKE.

O, KING, THIS TALK OF YOURS IS NOTHING BUT MADNESS!

IF YOU'RE BENT ON GOING BACK, GO . . . BUT I, DIOMED, AND ALL THE OTHER GREEKS WILL STAY TILL WE'VE TAKEN THE CITY OF TROY!

AND THEN HE TOOK BRISEIS. LET HIM KEEP HER IF HE WILL, BUT LET HIM NOT ASK ME FOR AID. THERE ARE OTHERS WHOM HE HAS NOT WRONGED AND SHAMED THUS . . . LET HIM ASK THEM HOW TO KEEP THE FIRE FROM THE SHIPS.

AS FOR HIS DAUGHTER, WHOM HE WOULD GIVE TO BE MY WIFE, I WOULD NOT MARRY HER . . . THOUGH SHE WERE AS BEAUTI- FUL AS APHRODITE HERSELF.

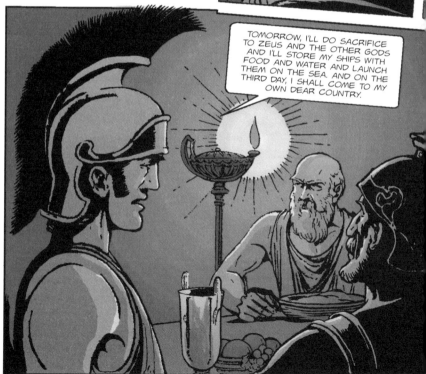

TOMORROW, I'LL DO SACRIFICE TO ZEUS AND THE OTHER GODS AND I'LL STORE MY SHIPS WITH FOOD AND WATER AND LAUNCH THEM ON THE SEA. AND ON THE THIRD DAY, I SHALL COME TO MY OWN DEAR COUNTRY.

I HEAR FOOTSTEPS COMING OUR WAY.

LET HIM PASS BY, THAT WE MAY TAKE HIM.

DIOMED AND ULYSSES LAY DOWN AMONG THE DEAD UNTIL DOLON PASSED BY THEM.

DOLON WAS CONFUSED AT THE SOUND OF THE MEN COMING TOWARD HIM . . .

HECTOR HAS SENT MEN AFTER ME TO RETURN.

DON'T KILL ME. MY FATHER WILL PAY A GREAT REWARD. HECTOR PERSUADED ME TO GO, PROMISING ME THE CHARIOT AND HORSES OF ACHILLES.

WHERE'S HECTOR? WHAT WATCH DOES THE TROJAN KEEP?

DOLON TALKED FOR HIS LIFE . . .

THERE ARE NO WATCHES SET, EXCEPT IN THAT PART OF THE CAMP WHERE HECTOR IS. THE ALLIES SLEEP WITHOUT WATCHES, THINKING THE TROJANS WILL DO THIS FOR THEM.

ULYSSES AND DIOMED DECIDED IT WAS PRUDENT TO SLAY DOLON.

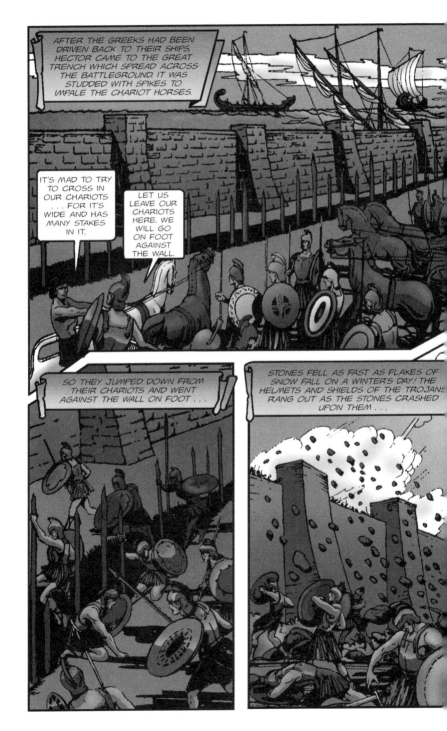

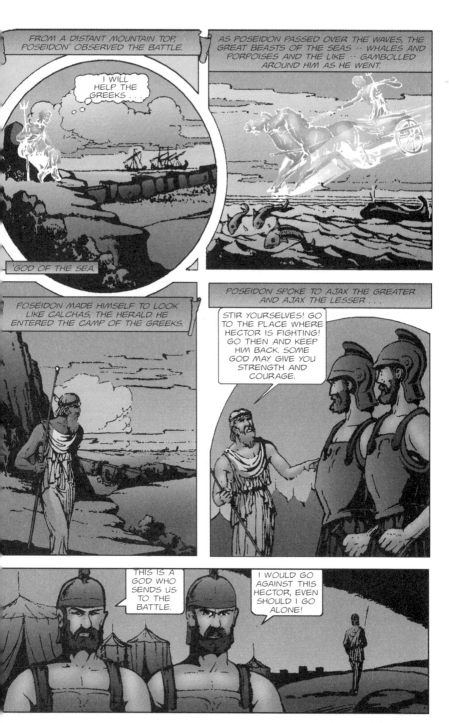

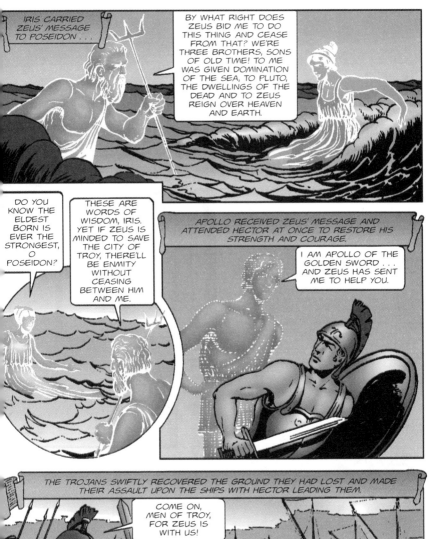

IRIS CARRIED ZEUS' MESSAGE TO POSEIDON...

BY WHAT RIGHT DOES ZEUS BID ME TO DO THIS THING AND CEASE FROM THAT? WE'RE THREE BROTHERS, SONS OF OLD TIME! TO ME WAS GIVEN DOMINATION OF THE SEA, TO PLUTO, THE DWELLINGS OF THE DEAD AND TO ZEUS REIGN OVER HEAVEN AND EARTH.

DO YOU KNOW THE ELDEST BORN IS EVER THE STRONGEST, O POSEIDON?

THESE ARE WORDS OF WISDOM, IRIS. YET IF ZEUS IS MINDED TO SAVE THE CITY OF TROY, THERE'LL BE ENMITY WITHOUT CEASING BETWEEN HIM AND ME.

APOLLO RECEIVED ZEUS' MESSAGE AND ATTENDED HECTOR AT ONCE TO RESTORE HIS STRENGTH AND COURAGE.

I AM APOLLO OF THE GOLDEN SWORD... AND ZEUS HAS SENT ME TO HELP YOU.

THE TROJANS SWIFTLY RECOVERED THE GROUND THEY HAD LOST AND MADE THEIR ASSAULT UPON THE SHIPS WITH HECTOR LEADING THEM.

COME ON, MEN OF TROY, FOR ZEUS IS WITH US!

BRING ME FIRE THAT WE MAY BURN THE SHIPS OF THESE ROBBERS, FOR ZEUS HAS GIVEN US THE VICTORY TODAY.

AJAX FOUGHT BRAVELY, THRUSTING AT ANYONE WHO CAME NEAR THE SHIPS WITH FIRE.

YOU MUST ACQUIT YOURSELVES AS MEN, O GREEKS. OUR HOPE IS IN COURAGE! THERE'S NO ONE TO SAVE YOU IF YOU'LL NOT SAVE YOURSELVES!

PATROCLUS ENTREATED ACHILLES TO HELP HIM SAVE THE GREEKS.

LET ME PUT ON YOUR ARMOUR AND LET YOUR PEOPLE GO WITH ME. THE TROJANS WILL THINK YOU'VE COME TO BATTLE AND THE GREEKS WILL HAVE A BREATHING SPACE!

GO, AND KEEP THE FIRE FROM THE SHIPS BUT WHEN YOU HAVE DONE THIS COME BACK AND FIGHT NO MORE WITH THE TROJANS.

AT THE SIGHT OF PATROCLUS, WHOM THEY BELIEVED TO BE ACHILLES, THE TROJANS FLED. THEN, PATROCLUS FORGOT ACHILLES' COMMAND.

NOW I SHALL TAKE THE CITY OF TROY!

GO BACK, PATROCLUS. IT'S NOT FOR YOU TO TAKE THE GREAT CITY OF TROY. NO, NOR EVEN ACHILLES, WHO IS A FAR BETTER MAN THAN YOU!

THREE TIMES DID PATROCLUS CHARGE INTO THE RANKS OF THE TROJANS AND EACH TIME HE SLEW NINE WARRIORS.

HECTOR SPOKE TO HIS CHARIOTEER.

WE'LL SEE WHETHER WE CAN NOT DRIVE BACK THIS PATROCLUS, FOR IT MUST BE HE. ACHILLES HE IS NOT, THOUGH HE WEAR HIS ARMOUR!

PATROCLUS STRUCK HECTOR'S CHARIOTEER WITH A GREAT ROCK.

AH, SEE HOW NIMBLE IS THIS MAN! SEE HOW WELL HE DIVES!

THE GOD APOLLO, ENRAGED AT PATROCLUS, STRUCK HIM A GREAT BLOW SO THAT HE COULD NOT SEE. THEN, ONE OF THE TROJANS WOUNDED PATROCLUS IN THE BACK.

AS PATROCLUS STOOD DEFENSELESS, HECTOR DROVE A SPEAR INTO HIM AND HE FELL TO THE GROUND . . .

DID YOU THINK, PATROCLUS, THAT YOU WOULD TAKE OUR CITY, SLAY US WITH THE SWORD, AND CARRY AWAY OUR WIVES AND DAUGHTERS?

LO! I'VE OVERCOME YOU WITH MY SPEAR AND THE FOWLS OF THE AIR SHALL EAT YOUR FLESH! EVEN GREAT ACHILLES CAN NOT HELP YOU.

YOU BOAST TOO MUCH, O HECTOR. IT'S APOLLO WHO HAS BROUGHT ME TO MY DEATH.

THE MEN OF BOTH SIDES FOUGHT OVER THE BODY OF PATROCLUS AND HECTOR STRIPPED THE BODY OF ACHILLES' ARMOUR AND WORE IT HIMSELF.

IN THE TENT OF ACHILLES . . .

I BRING BAD NEWS . . . PATROCLUS IS DEAD. AND HECTOR HAS HIS ARMS, BUT THE GREEKS AND TROJANS ARE FIGHTING FOR HIS BODY!

THETIS, HIS MOTHER, ATTENDED ACHILLES IN HIS GREAT DESPAIR.

WHY DO YOU WEEP, MY SON?

ALL THAT YOU ASKED FROM ZEUS, HE HAS DONE . . . BUT PATROCLUS IS DEAD. I DO NOT WISH TO LIVE BUT TO AVENGE MYSELF UPON HECTOR.

DO NOT SPEAK SO, FOR IT IS WRITTEN THAT WHEN HECTOR DIES, THE HOUR IS ALSO NEAR WHEN YOU MUST DIE!

I WOULD THAT I COULD DIE THIS HOUR, FOR I SENT MY FRIEND TO HIS DEATH! CURSED BE THE ANGER THAT SETS MEN TO STRIVE WITH ONE ANOTHER . . . AND AS FOR MY FATE, WHAT MATTERS IT?

THETIS VISITED THE TENT OF ACHILLES. SHE TOLD HIM THAT ZEUS WAS ANGERED BY ACHILLES' TREATMENT OF THE BODY OF HECTOR.

'TIS THE WILL OF ZEUS THAT YOU GIVE UP THE BODY TO KING PRIAM.

LET IT BE SO IF THE GODS WILL HAVE IT.

EDITOR'S NOTE: WITH THE FUNERAL OF HECTOR, HOMER'S ILIAD ENDS. WHAT HAPPENED AFTERWARD, WE LEARN FROM OTHER SOURCES.

LATER, AN ARROW FROM THE BOW OF PARIS, GUIDED BY THE GOD APOLLO, KILLED ACHILLES. IT WAS AN ARROW ALSO THAT TOOK THE LIFE OF PARIS, WHO CAUSED ALL THE TROUBLE.

THEN IT WAS THAT THE GREEKS DEVISED THE PLAN OF BUILDING A WOODEN HORSE . . . HIDING IN IT, IN ORDER TO EFFECT THEIR ENTRY INTO THE CITY. THE TROJANS DRAGGED THE HORSE INTO THE CITY, THINKING IT WAS AN OFFERING TO THE GODS. THUS THE GREEKS, EMERGING FROM THE HORSE, FINALLY TOOK THE CITY IN THE TENTH YEAR OF THE SIEGE.

THE END

THE ILIAD

HOMER

The tales in *Iliad* and the *Odyssey* [...] n western literature as we know it, sur- [...] ng some five hundred years, passed [...] storyteller to storyteller orally, until [...] er wrote them down in the middle of [...] 7th century BC. These tales tell us of a [...] society where warriors competed for [...] y, where gods and men struggled on [...] ly equal footing, and where many of [...] culture's defining values (honor, [...] age, self-knowledge, and heroism) were [...]. As early works, the *Iliad* and the *...ssey* provide a number of "foundation" ...es that have become staples of western ...ature. They also have preserved a way ...orytelling (oral composition) that is lost ...e a society develops its own written lit- ...y language; in a very real sense, the ...*d* and the *Odyssey* are "fossils" of a kind ...omposition that we can no longer cre-

There are many reasons to [...] and study these works: the [...] ...es themselves are enormous- [...] ...ntertaining, and have pro- [...] ...dly shaped our own cultural [...] ...tity by exploring hard ques- [...] ...s of what it means to be [...] ...an. But more than that, they [...] ...us to see three different sub- [...] ...eties: the Mycenean world [...] ...t which Homer writes, Homer's own [...] ld at the start of the Classical Age, and, [...] ...ourse, our own.

The *Iliad* (literally, the war for Ilos, or ...y), gives us two great stories folded into ... epic tale: the public tragedy of war in all its gruesome and violent detail, and the private tragedy of the hero Achilles. In the *Iliad*, men die in every way imaginable at the grim hands of the god of war, and for all the heroism it records, the text never loses sight of the cost of war, of the terrible waste in the loss of even a single life. The culture captured in this work required that its heroes pursue excellence—called "arete"— in all things. So warriors on both sides of this war needed their exploits to be recognized: to crush their opponents, to crow over their bodies and take their armor as prize. Homer's heroes are pragmatic, focused, and intense, but they are also human—with clearly stated fears and mis- givings. The heroic code compels them to fight, often to die; but they die knowing why they are fighting. As the Trojan hero Sarpedon remarks to his friend Glaukos in Book XII: "But now, seeing that the spirits of death stand close about us/in their thousands, no man can turn aside nor escape them,/let us go on and win glory for ourselves, or yield it to others." In Homer's *Iliad* the code for the heroes is unrelenting, rigorous and often unbelievably costly, but it is also defining and meaningful. Agamemnon, Hektor, Odysseus, and Diomedes know who they are and why they act as they do; in meeting the challenges and horrors of war, in pursuing excellence, these heroes know themselves.

There has always been a Troy. Its geography alone has defined its existence and secured its central role in the history of Western Civilization. Positioned at the mouth of the Dardanelle Straits and strategically controlling trade and access to the Bosphorous Sea, Troy existed before there was recorded history. Homer's Troy dates from about 1180 BC, at the end of the historical period known as the Mycenean Age (1600-1150). This Troy shows extensive damage by fire and its destruction (the subject matter of many works, the *Iliad* chief among them), marks the end of this period. Troy, immortalized in the Homeric epics and in the plays of the Classical Greek tragedians, is not a curiosity of literary or mythological invention; its fall marked the end of an entire civilization. Troy fell to the Mycenean Greeks and their pro-Hellenic gods, but all of this society, Greeks and Trojans alike, fell to what historians label the Dorian Invasion—a displacement of the Mycenean Greeks by more primitive and uncivilized Greek tribes who mostly obliterated their culture and created a "dark age" that lasted five hundred years.

The stories of Homeric Troy are survivors, because they were passed down generation by generation before they even came to Homer who wrote (we think) somewhere around 750 BC. The Myceneans did not have a written language (in our sense) and the more primitive Dorians barely had a culture, let alone an artistic sensibility; thus, the evolution of these texts (the *Iliad* and the *Odyssey*) is an extraordinary occurrence. Homer's epics have exerted an incomparable influence on Western Civilization for over three millennia; th collection of these stories, their transmi sion over centuries and their transforma from oral poetry to written text is the fi third of this remarkable journey.

It takes a supreme effort of t imagination for us to envision the cultural and artistic life of the Myceneans. Theirs was a comple and relatively sophisticated socie a network of independent monarc loosely joined by a shared histori and tribal identity. These people were expert builders, delicate craftsmen, and ly evolved in terms of social hierarchies political and economic realities, and mo and religious sensibilities. Their culture heir to strong Egyptian and Minoan infl ences (an earlier but no less sophisticate Greek culture based on the island of Cre with its legendary king Minos, circa 18 BC). The stories and legends and myths the Myceneans incorporated some of th earliest and most primitive elements and artifacts of all of Western Civilization. 1 historical and archeological timeline in Homeric texts is truly amazing: Homer writes five hundred years after the even describes took place, but his stories hav been handed down to him orally and include elements that predate (often sig cantly) the Mycenean culture he describ And there is not a written word anywhe this process, anywhere in this amazing j ney over the centuries, until Homer him sets stylus to papyrus.

It's a challenge for us to imagine th creative process of oral poetry, so straig jacketed are we by graphics, text, and th written word. Homer's final draft numbe thousands of lines, and his basic storyli and characters existed (without the bene of being written down) for hundreds of

Terms

ete: excellence in all things.

isteia: great success as a gift of the gods.

e: blindness of the soul; delusion.

iasmus: a word, even a story, told backward to emphasize meaning (as Kleopatra/Patroklos).

ctyl: in poetry, a unit of three beats, the first accented, the second and the third unaccented: **ca**refully.

ctylic Hexameter: six dactyls per line of poetry: **wan**dering **ang**rily **through**out the **coun**tryside **with**out his **char**iot….

ic simile: complex extended comparison that helps the reader to visualize what's going on.

ithet: phrase describing a character, that would also fill up a poetic line: "long-haired Menelaos" or "Zeus of the wide brows."

ocation: an opening prayer to the Muse of epic poetry for inspiration.

radeigma: stories with a "moral" that teach good behavior and wise decision-making.

ondee: in poetry, a unit of two beats, both accented: **my name.**

rs. How the plot and characters were ed along leads us to the essence of oral position, an art form as old as human ure which thrives on memory, formulaic ages, and poetic rhythm. It is the ain of the rhapsodes, professional court ers whose job it was to record, cata- e, and re-create the legendary and iliar stories of heroes and gods. In the neric texts we have in written form *one*

version of the Trojan War, one rendering of the return of the heroes after Troy. But there were probably thousands; each poet told his own version, making the familiar new and different, working and re-working the standard material from the same basic toolbox: no notes, just the familiar stories, the memorized and formulaic passages (component building blocks, puzzle pieces to be fit together), and meter.

THE POEM

All Classical Greek, including the Ionic dialect spoken by Homer, is *inflect-ed:* the function of a word is determined, not by where it falls in a sentence, but by its ending. A noun, depending on its ending, can be a subject, an object, etc.; likewise, a verb can be a predicate, a participle, or an infinitive with the change of an ending. It's crucial to understand how this affected the process of oral composition: the poet could manipulate the text by rhythm and beat, by *inflection*. Greek epic poets used *dactylic hexameter* lines—six predominantly dactylic feet, with spondees mixed in for variety and pacing (see **Terms**). This set rhythm was the first building block in composition: Classical Greek is a dactylic language, and the poets were quick to shape and repeat words and then groups of words which "automatically" made up parts of lines or whole lines or even whole sections of the poem. These "blocks" were easy to memorize and manipulate, and blocks could conveniently be plugged in as the story-telling demanded. Thus, names in the text are almost invariably tied to *epithets* (see **Terms**); these (and hundreds of other examples) show us the basics of how the poetry got built: lines made of combinations of dactyls or spondees (six units per line), easily memorized and flexibly interchangeable.

What's true for individual words and phrases is also true for individual lines, for larger set sequences of lines. Commonplace actions (dawning of the day, dressing, feasting, etc.) are set pieces, neatly packaged so they can be plugged in while the poet, thinking on his feet, decides spontaneously where to go next. A beginning or inexperienced reader may view these repetitions and set pieces as liabilities; in fact, they're the means by which a poet can create a piece as long and as complex as the *Iliad* without notes or writing.

The *Iliad* actually covers only about a month's worth of action in the ninth year of the ten-year war. We assume that other epics worked over other parts of the story, but for all the epic "sweep" of the *Iliad,* Homer keeps the focus pretty tightly on the story of the anger of Achilles and its devastating consequences. After a brief *invocation* (see **Terms**), Homer plunges directly into Achilles' confrontation with Agamemnon; starting in the middle of the story gives the work (for all its length and repetitiveness), astonishing immediacy.

Because his audience members were listeners rather than readers, Homer's narrative style was strong on "visuals." Much of the action in the text is strongly supported by *epic similes* (see **Terms**) and many of these similes use Nature as their subject matter: heroes are like ravenous lions, cunning leopards, or rampaging boars. Using Nature-based similes, Homer creates images of intense and surprising sophistication. Throughout the last third of the epic, for example, when Achilles' anger is at its most intense and devastating, he's described repeatedly as fire, making clear to even the most uneducated members of the audie the passion and destructiveness of his a Homer can craft a simile that isn't just tic but profound: in Book Six, the Troja warrior Glaukos meets the Greek hero Diomedes. As is often the case, the figh talk before the battle, and here Glaukos responds to the question of his family a heritage:

> ....*why ask of my generation?*
> *As is the generation of leaves, so*
> *is that of humanity.*
> *The wind scatters the leaves on the*
> *ground, but the live timber*
> *burgeons with leaves again in the*
> *season of the spring returning.*
> *So too the generation of men will*
> *grow while another*
> *dies.*
>
> Book VI, 145-150

This image—the contrast between the momentary world of man and the agele and immortal gods—is central to the u standing of the epic. It is an image that Homer repeats (Book XXI, 463-466) an one which he connects to the story's fir great, dramatic action (Achilles' dashin the scepter in the calamitous assembly Book I).

Once we get a feel for how oral co position works, it becomes easier to see how the poem is designed. Homer was master craftsman, taking many disparat parts (most of them probably not origin him) and shaping them, coordinating th into a focused and meaningful whole. S parts come from far outside the "domai of the text; the Catalogue of Ships in B II is obviously a set piece that Homer a to give his audience history and perspe on the conflict between Agamemnon an Achilles with which the story opens. A

ok X, which follows the powerful scene
the Embassy to Achilles, is another of
se set pieces; this self-contained story
hin a story—the spy mission
Odysseus and Diomedes—is
own as the Doloneia for its
tim, Dolon, who dies brutally
he hands of the two Greek
oes. In Book XVIII, there
urs another long block of set
ration, The Arms of Achilles.
st, in Book XXIII, Homer
lliantly paces the resolution

DOLON TALKED FOR HIS LIFE...

THERE ARE NO WATCHES SET, EXCEPT IN THAT PART OF THE CAMP WHERE HECTOR IS. THE ALLIES SLEEP WITHOUT WATCHES, THINKING THE TROJANS WILL DO THIS FOR THEM.

the war by separating the funeral of
roklos from the burial of Hektor with
ympic-style games Achilles holds in
nor of his fallen friend. These contests
den the perspective from the singular
us on the anger of Achilles and the allow
text to end on a quiet note.

The *Iliad* is a distinctly "moral" work,
e which asks questions about man's place
the world, and the meaning of his efforts.
is moral purpose shows in the conflict
l collaboration between gods and men, in
moral growth and development of indi-
ual characters, and in the consistent val-
s Homer defines in his portrait of this
cenean world. One type of formula
mer frequently employs—the
adeigma (see **Terms**)—demonstrates
s moral purpose. These stories, frequently
d by aged and wise counselors (Nestor,
am, Phoenix, and others), teach, and do
with great symmetry and balance. The
of paradeigma is everywhere in the text
l demonstrates both a high degree of
ral purpose *and* Homer's passionate
erest in symmetry and balance.

Perhaps the most powerful and mean-
ful of these paradeigma occurs in Book
of the *Iliad*, the Assembly to Achilles.
re, Phoenix, Achilles' own teacher,

comes as part of the delegation asking him
to put aside his anger. Along with magnificent gifts, Phoenix brings a story (Book,
IX, 525-599) about what hap-
pened to another great hero—
Meleagros—who refused to be
placated by gifts and petitions
offered in good faith by a suffering and ravaged people. That
hero could not be persuaded,
even by his wife Kleopatra;
only when it was too late did he
give in: the loss of life was
staggering and his honor was never fully
restored. This story does have an effect—a
slight one—on Achilles. But the kicker is in
the irony contained in the name of the
story's heroine; this Kleopatra has nothing
to do with the Egyptians or the Nile; it is
her name—actually the reversing of her
name—that matters most. Kleopatra backwards (in a device known as *chiasmus*—see
Terms) is Patroklos (Kleo/patra vs.
Patro/klos) whose death is the single most
important dramatic turning point in the second half of the epic.

STRUCTURE

The *Iliad* is an intensely structured and
carefully designed work which can be bro-
ken down into four large sections (Books I-
VIII: Achilles' anger and the consequences
of his withdrawal from battle; Books IX-
XVII: the failure of the Assembly and the
continuing devastation of Achilles' anger;
Books XVIII-XXII: Achilles' revenge of
Patroklos; and Books XXIII-XXIV: restora-
tion and insight). This order stresses the
dramatic and tragic elements of the story.
There is the initial conflict and its consequences, followed at the midpoint by an

intensifying of the conflict and a further heightening of the consequences. At the end there is a resolution, which restores the order that was disrupted by the opening crisis and gives Achilles a chance to learn from his experiences. And structure isn't limited to effective story-telling: chiasmus figured strongly in the elements of Phoenix's speech to Achilles (Kleopatra/Patroklos); there is an important chiasmatic arrangement linking together the first and the last books in the text. Scholars note that the opening and closing books of the epic share the same five themes, with the latter book essentially repeating the themes in reverse order. Thus, the entire story is framed to stress the symmetry of the epic, while the reverse order of themes demonstrates the development that has taken place over the course of the tale. Such careful construction is characteristic of the *Iliad* , without question a work of great logic, seamless artistry, and powerful sophistication.

> BEFORE A DOOR TO THE WALL LAY A GREAT STONE, SCARCELY TWO MEN COULD LIFT IT, BUT HECTOR TOOK IT UP AS EASILY AS A SHEPHERD CARRIES FLEECE OF A SHEEP, AND THREW IT . . .

CHARACTERS

The Greeks

Agamemnon: King of Mycenae and commander of the Greek forces.
Menelaos: King of Lacedaemon and Agamemnon's brother; Helen's husband.
Achilles: King of Phthia, leader of the Myrmidons. The greatest warrior of the Greeks.

Patroklos: Achilles' companion.
Odysseus: King of Ithaca; famed for his wiliness.
Ajax (the Great): from Salamis (there's another Ajax in the *Iliad*: the Oilean Ajax the Lesser).
Diomedes: King of Argos.
Helen: Wife of Menelaos, daughter of Zeus, abducted by Paris and brought to Troy.

The Trojans
Priam: King of Troy, father of Hektor.
Hektor: leader of the Trojan armies; son of Priam.
Paris: Hektor's brother, Helen's abductor.
Sarpedon: King of Lycia, son of Zeus

The Gods
Zeus: ruler of the gods.
Hades: ruler of the underworld.
Hera: goddess of marriage.
Athene: goddess of wisdom.
Poseidon: god of the sea.
Aphrodite: goddess of love.
Apollo: god of the arts.
Ares: god of war.

THE STORY PART

After the Invocation, Homer plunges directly into the story. Agamemnon, the of men and leader of the Greek forces, arrogantly refused a ransom offer from a Trojan priest of Apollo for the return of daughter Chryseis. Apollo answers the

> WAS THERE EVER A KING WHO HAD SUCH COWARDS FOR HIS PEOPLE?

priest's prayers, sending a plague upon Greek camp. After nine days of suffering and destruction, Achilles calls an

Achilles' Heel

According to legend, Achilles' mother Thetis, hearing that her son was doomed to an early death, dipped him into the River Styx (the river that separated the earth from the afterlife) to make him invulnerable, holding him by one heel. It worked—except for that one heel. In a sense, though, Achilles' *Achilles' heel* is really the pride and blindness that drives him to rage against Agamemnon.

embly, and with
et diplomacy,
ises the return
he girl to her
er (Chryseis,
h her name
ered to Cressida,
he subject of
er myth and
nance—notably
akespeare's play
*ilus and
essida*).
amemnon refus-
threatening to
p Achilles of his own prize, Briseis, for
's intimidated by Achilles' greatness. How
he be the "king of kings" if *his* war
ze is not the best? Here is the first great
me of the *Iliad*, the consequence of even
nomentary loss of balance, of a mistake
judgment. Agamemnon, as Homer por-
ys him, is an excellent fighter and a rea-
ably effective leader. At this moment,
wever, he has made a mistake, and in his
ndness (*ate*: see **Terms**) he can't find a
y out of his difficulties.
ere's no premeditation
re, just war weariness, the
ain of command, and the
ars laying siege to Troy—
erything and nothing.
t Agamemnon's decision
attack when challenged
the assembly spells disas-
for the Greek cause.

Homer stresses the consequences that
m from human decisions by comparing
: lives of mortal men with the existence
the immortal gods. The comparison is
t a flattering one for Homer's gods, who
: like petulant children, willful and mean-
rited. They play favorites, jump sides,

provoke, plot, and play with a total indifference to consequences. They can't die, so consequence doesn't touch them. No wonder there is such a high premium placed by the human heroes on reputation: unlike the gods who are ageless and immortal, humans inevitably die. *How* one dies therefore matters greatly. The *Iliad* is not, as some people mistakenly claim, the "Bible" of the Greeks, because the gods here aren't moral in our sense of the word. What matters here is what happens on the human plane, where individuals are tested by combat and crisis and come to a greater understanding of what makes them human.

Achilles himself is the embodiment of human perfection, the most accomplished, the best fighter, the fastest, the most gifted, blessed with one divine parent and extraordinary gifts and talents. He's feared by the Trojans and respected by his fellow Greek kings. He's not a one-dimensional character: he has intellectual talents and artistic gifts equal to his physical abilities. With these achievements comes a strong sense of his honor and status in the military hierarchy. When confronted by Agamemnon in the assembly, Achilles can't tolerate even a threat to his possessions, privilege or property. As the greatest warrior, Achilles can't—and won't—allow his reputation to

NEVER WAS THERE A KING SO SHAMELESS AND SO GREEDY! I HAVE BEEN FIGHTING AGAINST THE TROJANS FOR YOUR SAKE AND YOUR BROTHER'S. THEY NEVER DID HARM TO ME OR MINE.

GO, AND TAKE YOUR PEOPLE WITH YOU. BUT MARK, THE GIRL BRISEIS, WHO WAS GIVEN YOU, I WILL TAKE!

be diminished. Achilles declares that he will withdraw from fighting and, by doing so, allow the Trojans to be successful. Achilles' declaration makes clear what he believes is important: his honor, his reputation, his *arete*.

Agamemnon's momentary loss of judgment and Achilles' withdrawal from combat sets off a flurry of activity. Book One itself ends with Thetis, Achilles' mother and a sea nymph, petitioning Zeus to intervene on Achilles' behalf to see that Agamemnon and the rest of the Greeks are punished. Zeus, the father of the gods, has trouble with this request, because Olympus is already split into warring factions over the Trojan War; his wife Hera leads the pro-Greek faction, and he'll have no end of difficulties if he grants this request. In juxtaposing Olympus against Troy, Homer contrasts the realms of the divine and human. For Zeus this war is a source of domestic squabbles; for Achilles it is a crisis that defines his *life*. Book One concludes with a scene of comic relief, with Zeus artfully soothing Hera, trying to hide his intentions. And when all else fails, he can bluster and threaten. This low comedy reinforces the idea that the real action of the *Iliad* happens on earth, where decisions and choices have inevitable and often intense consequences.

As a first part of his plan to grant glory to Achilles at the expense of the Greeks, Zeus sends an evil dream to Agamemnon. The King is to test the army with classic reverse psychology; he's to offer to go home at once, give up the war and retreat. While the idea for this strategy comes from Zeus, it's really all about Agamemnon—playing on the insecurity that originally caused the epic's opening dramatic action. Blindly self-centered, Agamemnon badly misreads the attitude of his warriors; confused and distraught by the public brawl for justice that they have witnessed in assembly, and frightened by Achilles' harsh words and his withdrawal from battle, they rush to leave. only some quick thinking Odysseus that saves the day His humiliation of Thersites (the only common man in the text) distracts the army and restores both morale and order. But it's clear at this point that all the Greeks (neatly catalogued in the second half of this book) will suffer because of the humiliation of Achilles.

Because Homer works on an epic canvas, the actual disaster that will befall the Greeks happens slowly, built with methodical inevitability. Such a pacing places a greater emphasis and focus on the human actors (as opposed to the gods); Homer waits to develop the details of the tragedy of Achilles. Instead, he shows us a full day of combat so that we may see the horrors of war in the fullest possible way, and so that we may understand what it means for Achilles, the code's greatest practitioner and the model of its values, to choose not to fight. Achilles will be "replaced" by Diomedes (Diomeds in the CI version) and this "master hero in training" will have a brilliantly successful day until he's wounded (in the foot, a scary foreshadowing of Achilles' own death: shot in the heel with an arrow). But Diomedes' success only reminds us of what has been lost by Achilles' withdrawal from combat; he's truly conspicuous by his absence, and the

WHEN THE TWELVE DAYS OF THE FEASTING WERE OVER, THETIS ROSE OUT OF THE SEA AND WENT TO OLYMPUS.

O FATHER ZEUS, AGAMEMNON HAS SHAMED MY SON, ACHILLES! DO THOU, THEREFORE, MAKE THE TROJANS PREVAIL IN BATTLE SO THAT THE GREEKS FIND THEY CAN NOT DO WITHOUT ACHILLES.

er he stays out, the worse it will be for Greeks.

From Book III through to Book VIII, dramatic action sweeps across the dusty n of Troy; we begin now to see how bat is conducted and we are gradually oduced to the Trojans. In Book III we t Helen of Troy in all her seductive m; even the old men of Troy, exhausted close to despair, acknowledge her beau-nd even defend the war: hers *is* "the that launched a thousand ships." We see the hero of Troy, Hektor. Champion he city and a bold and reckless fighter, tor's motives are the antithesis of illes'; Homer makes clear that he's a of the people: civic-minded, patient, rant, responsible, just. Although he erstands and subscribes also to the hero-ode, Hektor clearly fights for something ond personal honor. In a poignant and ous scene in Book VI, Homer shows us

tor with his ily. About to art for battle, tor comforts wife dromache his son yanax, who sts into tears, htened by his father's helmet. He con-s his wife by appealing to her sense of c responsibility: he fights to avoid me, to protect his parents and the city, to do what he has to do, "since I have ned to be valiant" (Bk. VI, 444). Then asually scoops his son up in arms, takes his terrifying helmet, and laughs away boy's tears. Mindful of and responsive to needs of others, this Hektor is unlike hero in the Greek Camp; he provides a trast and a counterweight to Achilles'

intense, inward-looking concentration. He's a worthy opponent, although he's no equal to Achilles in strength or skill (he'd rank about sixth overall in a catalogue of fighters). Through all these elements—the catalogue of ships, the interplay between the gods and men, the sweep of combat from the Greek Camp to the Walls of Troy, the studied contrast between the principal combatants—Homer is able to expand the scope and range of the narrative and examine individual versus group behavior.

To stress this point, Homer makes all of his combats individual battles; no army bears down to attack the other; instead, one hero emerges to challenge another. Even in the sweeping movement of strategic attack and retreat, Homer keeps us focused on the individual heroes and their personal successes and failures. This approach places great priority on the heroic code and the pursuit of arete, but it also personalizes the war in a way that is striking, even shocking, to first time readers. Most readers think of the *Iliad* as a poem which glorifies war. But Homer is deeply aware of the costs of war and the achievement of reputation. Homer is remarkably accurate in detailing how many ways men can die in battle; gaping gashes, spraying blood, and gruesome injuries enliven the reporting of the individual combats, not in celebration of violence but in a sober and realistic portrait of the suffering, loss and grief that arises when men fight. There's always a sense that it is the old and the helpless who really suffer in war. If Hektor dies in battle *his* suffering will be at an end; Astyanax and Priam, Andromache and all the other Trojans will face the destruction of their city, the slaughter of the innocent, helpless and aged. In this first section of the text, the theme is war itself: what it has done to the Greeks over their ten years laying siege to the city, and what it has done to the Trojans watching the hope for their city's survival fade over those ten years.

Book VIII ends with the Greeks penned tightly within the hastily constructed defensive perimeter of their camp. The Trojans, led by Hektor, are camped outside the walls, and their fires "blazed numerous around them." The Trojans have won considerable success on the battlefield; slowly, inevitably, Zeus's decision to honor Achilles has yielded a concrete plan of action. Zeus has ordered the other gods to stay out of the fighting (at least overtly; a don't ask, don't tell sort of policy). The long first day of fighting has ended; the dead have been retrieved and honored, the fortifications around the ships have been secured, and the Greeks watch nervously through the night. Their leaders have done their best under the circumstances, but many are deeply troubled; without Achilles, the defeat of Troy seems unlikely in the extreme.

THE STORY PART 2

The second section opens with one of the most famous and well-known scenes from all of Greek literature, the Embassy to Achilles. Understanding this scene is cr cial to our appreciation of the text, beca in it Achilles undergoes a major change becoming more complex as we watch. book is also a major crossroad for man the other important themes in the epic: the destruction of the Greeks by the Tro

A THOUSAND FIRES WERE BURNING, AND BY EACH FIRE SAT FIFTY MEN. AND THE HORSES STOOD BY THE CHARIOTS CHAMPING OATS AND BARLEY. SO THEY ALL WAITED FOR MORNING . . .

has reached a critical mass; here, the w concept of the heroic code is examined searing dramatic detail; and here the dir tion the rest of the story will take is det mined. The book opens with Agamemn making a public admission that his earli action was ill-advised, a madness of the soul; it ends with Achilles' yielding slig in respons Agamemn gifts and t pleas of h friends an comrades. his self-imposed e from battle, Achilles has clearly done so thing more than wallow in self-pity; he examined his life deeply. Because so m of his identity has been as a warrior, his self-examination has led Achilles to exa ine the whole heroic code on which his society is based. His thoughts—about li and death and their meaning—are the m profound and complex in the text. As Achilles speaks to his friends, it's clear no one in this story has thought more

ZEUS TOOK A HAND IN THE STRUGGLE AND ADDRESSED THE GODS AND GODDESSES . . .

LISTEN AND OBEY! NO ONE OF YOU SHALL HELP EITHER THE GREEKS OR THE TROJANS . . . AND MARK THIS . . . IF ANY GOD OR GODDESS DARES TO DO SO, I'LL THROW HIM DOWN INTO THE OUTER DARKNESS!

...ly about the hard questions of what it
...ns to be human.

The deepening of Achilles' character is
...arent when Odysseus,
...enix and Ajax find
... playing his lyre and
...ging one of the "old,
...ic" stories; he's more
...a fighting machine.
...ysseus lists the gifts
... Agamemnon offers as
...npensation for the
...lt Achilles suffered;
...h his usual guile he

WHAT PROFIT HAVE I HAD PUTTING MY LIFE IN PERIL DAY AFTER DAY? I TOOK TWELVE CITIES TO WHICH I TRAVELED IN SHIPS, AND ELEVEN TO WHICH I WENT BY LAND AND FROM ALL I CARRIED MUCH SPOIL...

...its any mention of submission to the
...ng as a condition of reconciliation. But
...hilles has little interest in gifts and com-
...nsation. First, he reminds Odysseus that
...e a person has been publicly humiliated
...stigma can never be completely erased;
...hout respect and honor, there is nothing
...t distinguishes the hero from the coward.
...hilles goes on, cataloguing his own
...ievement (including the 23 cities he per-
...nally destroyed), then wonders what all
...effort was for:

...For not
worth the value of my life are all
the possessions they fable
were won for Ilion, that strong-
founded citadel, in the old days
when there was peace, before the
coming of the sons of the
Achaians...
Of possessions
cattle and fat sheep are things to
be had for the lifting,
and tripods can be won, and the
tawny high heads of horses,
but a man's life cannot come back
again, it cannot be lifted
nor captured again by force, once
it has crossed the teeth's barrier.

The illusion of significance all heroes
live by is shattered for Achilles. Honor and
glory are hollow distinc-
tions, not worth living or
dying for. If what his mother
told him is true, he has two
destinies open to him: why
would he give up precious days
of life for reputation? What
Achilles will tell Odysseus in
the Underworld (in the
Odyssey) is true now:
"better to be a slave
to a slave to a man with no property than to
be an honored king over all the perished
dead." Achilles no longer defines himself
exclusively by his heroism and status. This
Achilles is infinitely more complex and
impressive because this Achilles has examined his life.

Where Odysseus appeals to Achilles'
pride as a great warrior, the next speaker,
his aged tutor Phoenix, makes a plea to
Achilles' emotional side. This appeal to
Achilles' heart—and guilt—puts him on the
defensive, and he literally pleads for mercy;
he's also moved by the argument (and the
guilt) and he makes the first of two conces-
sions: instead of leaving at dawn for home,
he will wait until the next day to decide on
a plan of action. After Ajax makes his
appeal—straightforward, pragmatic and
brief—Achilles bends further: he is still
angry but he won't leave. The Greeks have
gained something—but not enough. The
Trojans will continue to punish and pound
them (bringing Zeus' plan to completion),
and the events and actors that will shape the
tragedy of Achilles are set in motion. From
Achilles' decision to stay will come the
death of Sarpedon, the death of Patroklos,
and the death of Hektor.

The intensely inward focus of the Embassy's failure to persuade Achilles to return to battle is balanced by the contrasting events detailed in Book X. While this story-within-a-story is generally regarded as a set piece, it serves an important dramatic function here. The story tells of a successful spy mission conducted by Odysseus and Diomedes; they learn much of the Trojan encampment, they outwit and butcher the completely outmatched Trojan spy Dolon, and they capture the magnificent horses of Rhesos. Their success sets up the initial Greek successes that will happen with the next day's battle, while at the same time contrasting the previous scene's emotions of disappointment and despair. Homer understands that he has a long and complex story to tell, and he's attentive to pacing and dramatic tension.

ACTING ON THE INFORMATION OF THE SLAIN DOLON, DIOMED AND ULYSSES STOLE INTO THE TROJAN CAMP, AND AFTER SLAYING MANY WHO SLEPT, DEPARTED WITH A PRIZED CHARIOT . . .

The next day opens with a number of Greek successes. Stung by the aggressive forays of the Trojans, the Greeks mount a stalwart defense of their camp. Agamemnon, Odysseus, and Diomedes each have a time of *aristeia* (see **Terms**), where success comes easily on the field of battle. Each hero lives by the heroic rules outlined by Odysseus: "since I know that it is the cowards who walk out of the fighting,/but if one is to win honor in battle, he must by all means/stand his ground strongly, whether he be struck or strike another down" (Bk. XI, 408—410). But one by one, the heroes receive wounds that send them out of the battle (Diomedes

PATROCLUS ENTREATED ACHILLES TO HELP HIM SAVE THE GREEKS.

LET ME PUT ON YOUR ARMOUR AND LET YOUR PEOPLE GO WITH ME. THE TROJANS WILL THINK YOU'VE COME TO BATTLE AND THE GREEKS WILL HAVE A BREATHING SPACE!

GO, AND KEEP THE FIRE FROM THE SHIPS, BUT WHEN YOU HAVE DONE THIS, COME BACK AND FIGHT NO MORE WITH THE TROJANS.

takes one in the foot, making his paralle Achilles unmistakable). The tide of battl shifts once more, this time in favor of th Trojans. The fortification around the can is breached, and after much hard fightin Hektor sets to one of the Greek ships It's a bloody couple of books with some of the m ghastly fighting in the *Iliad*. Even Achill can't help but notice and become involve In spite of his supposed lack of interest i what happens to the Greeks under Agamemnon's command, he sends his be friend Patroklos to gather information, ar that's a fateful step.

Nowhere in the *Iliad* does Homer stress more poignantly and eloquently the terrible cost of war, the terrible waste of each life that is sacrificed, than in the pai and mirrored deaths of Sarpedon and Patroklos. Each man is decent and moral, concerned for others, loved by the gods, a deserving of a better fate. Sarpedon (see page **47**) gives voice to the single most articulate statement of why these heroes fight, so it's clea that he (and Patroklos) know exactly what the consequence of their actions are. Patroklos also has deep feelings and intense sympathies; when he hears Nestor's account of how badly the battle has turned against the Greeks, he fights back tears as he leaves the main camp to report the news to Achilles.

Patroklos begins a fateful sequence o action when he returns to Achilles' tent an begs Achilles "in his great innocence" (Bk

, 45) for permission to wear his armor, he chance that the mere presence of the ous armor on the field of battle will ten the Trojans and allow the Greeks gh breathing space to organize their nses and save their ships. Achilles ts the request; he is, after all a reason- man; he does care about his allies, and atroklos' friend mentor he s to deny him thing. But illes puts con- ons on the use is armor:

PATROCLUS STRUCK HECTOR'S CHARIOTEER WITH A GREAT ROCK.

AH, SEE HOW NIMBLE IS THIS MAN! SEE HOW WELL HE DIVES!

oklos is to fight defensively, just ugh to save the Greeks; under no cir- stances is he to take the offensive. In back of his mind Achilles hopes that the of them can defeat Troy together; ides, as good a fighter as Patroklos is, dangerous out there without Achilles to ch over him. In agreeing, Achilles offers rayer to Zeus for Patroklos' success and return; Zeus grants only the first uest.

Patroklos puts on the armor of hilles: what must it have felt like to ust the shoulder straps, to see the glint of sharp edge of the magnificent sword, to unt the chariot as the warrior flying into tle behind the divine horses, Xanthos and ios? Led by Patroklos, the Myrmidon ops plunge into battle, inspiring the war- ary Greeks. The perimeter of the camp is ckly secured and the Trojans are driven o the ditch; even Hektor scrambles into reat in the face of Patroklos' advance, for as if Zeus has granted him success in npensation for his impending death. roklos gets caught up in the heat of bat- and forgets the limits Achilles imposed him. In a near-miraculous leap, he

launches the chariot across the ditch and begins a wild pursuit of Hektor, an attack that will take him to the walls of Troy, and into conflict with Apollo himself.

Homer makes us care greatly for Patroklos, but Homer also makes his limits clear, as Patroklos oversteps his bounds, deluded and momentarily unbalanced by a blindness of the soul. As Apollo reminds him, "...it is not destined/that the city of the proud Trojans shall fall before your spear/ nor even at the hand of Achilles, who is far better than you are" (Bk. XVI, 707-710).

Patroklos can't kill Hektor (Achilles is fated to do so), but he does kill the hero Sarpedon. Sarpedon is a Trojan favorite, decent and humane; the calamity of his death is made clear by how closely involved Zeus himself becomes. Sarpedon is Zeus' son and the king of the gods is deeply trou- bled; he even contemplates saving Sarpedon from his day of destiny (if a man avoided his appointed death he would live forever). Hera chides her husband and—reluctantly —he agrees to let events play out as they have been foreordained, but he weeps "tears of blood" over the loss of his son.

Homer uses the death of Sarpedon to raise Patroklos' stature, but he does so in ways that underscore the shared bond of killer and victim (an important theme in its own right for the last sections of the text). Homer makes us care about Sarpedon; we know that he's a devout family man, that he's an articulate and thoughtful warrior, and that he's a bold and reckless fighter. The great triumph Patroklos achieves in slaughtering Sarpedon boosts his confi- dence and drives him further across the plain in search of Hektor. So Sarpedon's death begins a grim cycle of killer becoming victim: they fight now over his body; soon they will fight over the body of Patroklos, and then over the body of Hektor.

Having stripped Sarpedon's body of its glorious armor, Patroklos hunts for Hektor. (see previous page.) While Homer doesn't excuse Patroklos' arrogance, he doesn't forget his affection and sympathy for the man. Homer makes the death of Patroklos into a ritualized killing, with the gods so much a factor that Patroklos becomes someone special who's earned an unusual death, and someone whose death sends a clear message to Hektor. In his last words, Patroklos warns Hektor not to be as he has just been—heedless and arrogant—advice Hektor inevitably ignores. Of Patroklos Homer says, "the end of death closed in upon him,/and the soul fluttering free of his limbs went down into Death's house/mourning her destiny, leaving youth and manhood behind her" (Bk. XVI, 855-857).

The adrenaline rush of battle, the life and death finality of it, naturally makes it hard for any individual, even one like Hektor or Achilles, to stick to the Classical command urging moderation in all things. Patroklos can't find this balance as he stands over the body of Sarpedon, and Hektor can't keep himself from feeling triumphant as he strips Achilles' glorious armor from the shoulders of the slain Patroklos. It remains for Zeus—so distant from the struggles of men—to help us

with the perspective we need to have:

> *...Ah, poor wretch!*
> *There is no thought of death in*
> *your mind now, and yet death*
> *stands*
> *close beside you as you put on the*
> *immortal armor*
> *of a surpassing man. There are*
> *others who tremble before him*
> *Now you have killed this man's*
> *dear friend, who was strong*
>   *and gentle,*
> *and taken the armor, as you*
> *should not have done, from his*
> *shoulders*
> *and head. Still for the present I*
> *will invest you with great strength*
> *to make up for it that you will not*
> *come home out of the fighting,*
> *nor Andromache take from your*
> *hands the glorious armor of*
>   *Achilles.*

Book XVIII, 200-208

THE STORY PART

In all Achilles' thinking about the h ic code and about the value and direction his life, he never imagines that his praye for Patroklos' safety will not be granted.

More to the point, he nev expects that Patroklos wi disobey his orders. This s between expectation and outcome is the start of a process that will bring Achilles wisdom through suffering. He waits in the Myrmidon camp for Patroklos' triumphant ret while his friend's corpse in danger of desecration

THETIS, HIS MOTHER, ATTENDED ACHILLES IN HIS GREAT DESPAIR

WHY DO YOU WEEP, MY SON?

ALL THAT YOU ASKED FROM ZEUS, HE HAS DONE . . . BUT PATROCLUS IS DEAD. I DO NOT WISH TO LIVE BUT TO AVENGE MYSELF UPON HECTOR.

rojans, and Hektor now wears
lles' armor. Achilles, whose excellence
the standard for others, has no clue that
oklos has died and that all their plans
ther have come to nothing.

The news of Patroklos death all but
Achilles; it *does* destroy Achilles' idea
ho he is. Homer underscores this
ge by bringing Thetis into the scene to
fort her son as he rolls in the dust in
rief. (See previous page.)

ompanied by her sister nymphs, she
rns the grieving Achilles as if he's
dy dead. Achilles makes clear that he
now only for revenge, and if killing
tor means that he too will soon die, so
. With an intensity and focus that is
ost inhuman, Achilles returns to war,
ng up his feud with Agamemnon as if it
nothing, and prepared to give up his
also. Achilles ends the long day's battle
un in Book XI) by shouting his grief
readiness for revenge three times from
parapet of the defensive wall; the
ans are stunned and scattered by these
ts and give ground so that the Greeks
at least rescue the body of Patroklos
n the battle.

Hektor's day of
eia ends with
tfall, but like
oklos, he wants
e; he believes that
an carry the fight
ugh to a swift and
ble victory. The

s that Achilles has returned means to
, in this state, only an opportunity for
ater glory. His vainglory, fueled by his
nt successes, now compels him to take
Achilles, whose sole focus is revenge.
Achilles, his former anger and preoccu-
on with Agamemnon's insult has crys-

tallized into murderous rage at Hektor. It is
frightening to see Achilles in this state; he's
wild, barbaric, vowing to desecrate the
body of Hektor once he is dead, and to sacrifice twelve Trojan victims at the funeral
of Patroklos. The grim and heartless warrior waits only for the making of a new set
of armor, for he can't just borrow someone
else's equipment, and his own was taken by
Hektor.

Thetis, bowing to the inevitable, goes
to the gods to ask for divine armor for her
doomed son, and the poem moves from
Achilles to the magnificent home of the
god-smith Hephaistos. Homer details the
elaborate shield Hepahistos crafts, in
another of the set passages he has incorporated into his text, and it affords the narrative a key moment of perspective. This
divine armor does more than solve the
practical problem of replacing Achilles'
lost armor; it forces us to see Achilles'
struggles in the larger context of human
life. The new shield he takes into combat is
a work of art that details a comprehensive
look at all the Homeric world. This juxta-
position, where a world view is pictured on
a weapon of war, reminds
us that Achilles' preoccu-
pation with himself, with
his grief and anger, consti-
tutes only a small segment
of human life. The effec-
tiveness of such a juxtapo-
sition here is among the
most well-documented of

the many used in the *Iliad;* Homer takes a
set piece he found elsewhere and has
shaped it to fit the particular demands of
his own narrative. Without this scene we
would quickly hate this Achilles and be
frightened of him; his intensity and passion
are too much to handle.

Nothing matters to Achilles except killing Hektor; he doesn't care about the gifts that Agamemnon returns or the stammering apology he offers. Achilles doesn't care about food, drink or rest, and barely hears the lamentations of Briseis (now restored to him) as she weeps for Patroklos. He exhausts himself through the long night in intense grief over Patroklos' body as he struggles with "a sorrow beyond endurance" (Bk. XIX, 367). When, moments before his return to battle, his divine horses try to warn him off from the approaching battle, Achilles abruptly cuts them off saying, "I myself know well it is destined for me to die here/ far from my beloved father and mother. But for all that/ I will not stop till the Trojans have had enough of my fighting" (Bk. XIX, 421-423).

Achilles' return to war is a thing of terrible beauty. It's as if no other warrior were fighting on the Greek side. He sweeps the Trojans toward the river, and when there are no more Trojans to kill, he fights with the river itself. Achilles veers dangerously close to losing his humanity as he taunts his victims and slaughters them without mercy. One thing alone redeems Achilles here: his self-awareness. He knows that the price of revenge is his own death and he accepts that unconditionally. When the Trojan Lycaon throws himself at the hero's feet and petitions for mercy, Achilles answers not out of hatred but with a bond of friendship. There will be no mercy but there will also be no recriminations:

THE TROJANS WERE DRIVEN BACKWARDS BY THE FURY OF THE ASSAULT LED BY ACHILLES.

So, friend, you die also. Why all this clamor about it?
Patroklos also is dead, who was better by far than you are.
Do you not see what a man I am, how huge and splendid
And born of a great father and the mother who bore me immortal?
Yet even I have also my death and my strong destiny...
when some man in the fighting will take the life from me also.
Book XXI, 106-110, 112

In the end, Achilles finds his victim and, with Hektor's death, the wrath then fulfilled. We are reminded that to be human is to be flawed and that Hektor (like Sarpedon and Patroklos before him) deserves our sympathy more than our censure. Homer reminds us of Hektor's decency and nobility by showing us the consequences of his death for his parents, for family, and for his city. In the end, Hektor has no illusions left and he accepts the reality of his death at the hands of a better fighter. "But now my death is upon me. Let me at least not die without a struggle, inglorious,/but do some big thing first, that men to come shall know of it" (Book XXII, 303 -305).

In a poignant irony Hektor, wearing Achilles' armor, becomes his mirror image. Achilles kills Hektor savagely and without mercy; it's almost a shock to watch such cruelty and violence. What saves the moment is Achilles' sense of the moment, his awar

s of himself, of his place in the world.
h his dying words, Hektor warns
hilles not to go too far, not to become an
nse to the gods. Achilles answers sim-
: "Die: and I will take my own death at
atever time/Zeus and the rest of the
mortals choose to accomplish it" (Book
II, 365 -366).

Hektor dies, as Patroklos did, "leaving
ath and manhood behind," while Achilles
es for a little while longer. His savagery
played itself out. In a moment of quiet
lection not far from the end of the story,

hilles articulates
sad state of human
stence as he sees it.
says that Zeus has
urns from which
dispenses fortune
men, one with good
k, the other with
luck. Zeus usually
xes the ingredients,
that most men get
ne good fortune and some bad. No one,
hilles asserts, gets all good fortune, but
ne do get all bad. "Such is the way the
ds spun the life for unfortunate
rtals,/that we live in unhappiness, but the
ds themselves have no sorrow" (Book
IV, 525 -526). The immortals have no
es or worries; men do, but they also have
portunities for glory and excellence, rea-
able compensation for a transient life.

THE STORY PART 4

Homer quiets down the intensity and
us of the narrative quickly in Book
III. For Achilles himself, the destructive
otions of vengeance and violence are
rged by the funeral of Patroklos. The
sheer size of this event offers Achilles a
sense of closure as well as a chance to
accept Patroklos' death—and his own.
While Achilles remains the main focus of
this scene, Homer broadens the focus con-
siderably by contrasting Achilles' intense
and personal grief with the carefree attitude
of the gods. In addition, Homer also
widens the perspective by presenting in
Book XXIII an elaborate and extensive "set
piece" on the funeral games for Patroklos.
This mini-Olympics (with competition in a
variety of contests including running,

ACHILLES PIERCED THE ANKLE-BONES OF THE DEAD MAN AND FASTENED THE BODY WITH THONGS OF OX-HIDE TO THE CHARIOT.

wrestling, armed combat, chariot racing,
and boxing) re-acquaints us with the major
heroes and opens up the range and variety
of emotions and personalities (since the
text has been focused on the wrath of
Achilles). We see a different Achilles:
quiet, magnanimous—he smiles for the
first time in days—who has emerged not
only wiser and more understanding but also
spiritually and emotionally more mature.
While the other heroes strive for honor and
title, Achilles remains removed—dignified,
generous, and god-like; his is a greatness
defined by being.

One test remains for Achilles: what to
do with the body of Hektor. As most readers of the story know, Achilles in his
intense grief and anger not only kills his
rival but desecrates his body, dragging it

around the city for all to see. As favored as Achilles has been by the gods, such behavior is unacceptable, all the more so because in the eyes of the gods Hektor was a good, responsible and moral man. And so Zeus sends Priam, the aged King of Troy, to beg for the body of his son. Protected by the gods, Priam journeys into the Greek camp itself, a journey that is not unlike a journey to Hades itself. There at last the King meets the great warrior, saying "I have gone through what no other mortal on earth has gone through;/ I put my lips to the hands of the man who has killed my children" (Book XXIV, 505 -506). Achilles answers with words of comfort and consolation, for he sees in Priam his own father who will soon have to mourn the death of *his* son. Together the two weep, each for his own sorrows but more importantly for the sorrows they share, the sorrows of human life—its struggles, its transient nature, its risks and defeats. Achilles plays the part of the generous host, then helps the King prepare his son for transport. The epic itself ends quietly with the King leaving Achilles' tent under the cloak of darkness to begin the first of twelve days of mourning for his son Hektor. Achilles, in returning to himself, has returned to the good graces of the gods and to his rightful position as greatest of the Greeks, in new and better ways the embodiment of arete, excellence in all things.

STUDY QUESTIONS

•To us, Achilles' fury with Agamemnon may seem startlingly overblown. What about the society of the time explains his reaction?

•The gods interfere constantly in human affairs. Many of the fighters in the Iliad are referred to as "beloved by the gods" or "favored" by the gods. Does this actually work in their favor? Would you want to be "beloved by the gods" yourself? Why?

•What are the values the Mycenean society most valued? Do these values work for—or against—the characters?

•In all the *Iliad* Homer only mentions one character who is a commoner: Thersites, whom Odysseus humiliates to distract the troops from rebelling against Agamemnon. Why do you think there are no common soldiers in Homer's war story?

•Are there any circumstances in which you can imagine "oral transmission" of a story? What additions and distortions might there be? What does that suggest about the "accuracy" of Homer's facts on the *Iliad*? In the long run, is accuracy the most important factor in the story?

•There aren't many "women's roles" the *Iliad*—and many female characters are goddesses. What does the *Iliad* show you about *mortal* women in that society?

About the Essayist:

Maurice A. Randall holds a B.A. from Harvard University and an M.A. from Dartmouth University. He has taught Classics and English at the Roxbury Latin School for almost twenty years.